Deer Eat Buds and Leaves

Charmaine Robertson

Rosen REAL READERS

Rosen Classroom™
New York

This deer eats plants.

Plants taste good.

This deer eats buds.

They grow on trees.

This deer eats leaves.

Deer eat a lot!

Words to Know

buds

deer

leaves

trees